First Edition, July 1998.

ISBN 0-7363-0416-9

Published by

Living Stream Ministry
1853 W. Ball Road, Anaheim, CA 92804 U.S.A.
P. O. Box 2121, Anaheim, CA 92814 U.S.A.

Printed in the United States of America

98 99 00 01 02 03 / 9 8 7 6 5 4 3 2 1

CONTENTS

PREFACE

This book is a translation of messages given in Chinese by Brother Witness Lee in Anaheim, California in a fellowship with the elders from Taiwan, Hong Kong, and Malaysia on October 18-21, 1994.

work which He is carrying out includes: first, the work of sanctification (Col. 1:22; 1 Thes. 5:23); second, the work of renewing (Rom. 12:2; Titus 3:5); third, the work of transformation (2 Cor. 3:18); and fourth, the work of conformation (Rom. 8:29a). Finally, He as the life-giving Spirit will bring His people into glory (Heb. 2:10; Col. 3:4) so that their body will be redeemed and their entire being will be glorified (Phil. 3:21). At such a time, they will be exactly the same as the firstborn Son of God within and without—in life, in nature, in disposition, and in bodily form.

THE EMBODIMENT OF THE TRIUNE GOD

Here we need to see that the firstborn Son of God is the embodiment of the Triune God. First, God became flesh; second, this One in the flesh became the life-giving Spirit. Now this Spirit is the compound Spirit, the aggregate Spirit, and the consummation of the processed Triune God. Such a Spirit as the consummation of the Triune God works the Triune God into the entire being of the believers.

Hence, the processed Triune God is embodied in the all-inclusive Christ, and this Christ, who is the embodiment of the Triune God, has become the all-inclusive Spirit of the Triune God. Today the all-inclusive Christ as the embodiment of the Triune God has become the all-inclusive Spirit. This Triune God has been working in us since our regeneration and will continue until we are exactly the same as the firstborn Son of God. All of us as God's chosen ones need to pass through the processes of sanctification, renewing, transformation, and conformation unto the glorification of our entire being. We are in the processed Triune God for Him to work in us to the extent that we are exactly the same as the embodiment of God, the firstborn Son of God, so that we all may become the embodiment of God. The firstborn Son of God is the individual embodiment of God; we as the many sons of God are the corporate embodiment of God. The reality of this embodiment is the all-inclusive Spirit. When this embodiment is expressed, it is the Body of Christ.

You can see the church on this earth, but it is not easy for you to see the Body. What people call the church refers mostly to the gathering together of a group of believers of Christ to form an assembly. This is the *ekklesia,* the church, which is something visible. It is not easy, however, for people to see that the church is a matter of life. The consummation of this life aspect is the Body of Christ. How is this consummation carried out? It is carried out through regeneration, sanctification, renewing, transformation, conformation, and eventually, glorification.

THE CONSUMMATION OF THE BODY OF CHRIST—
THE NEW JERUSALEM

The Body of Christ consummates in the New Jerusalem. In other words, eventually, the Body of Christ becomes the New Jerusalem. The New Jerusalem is the conclusion of all these matters. Therefore, in the Bible, from Genesis to Revelation, the last thing that is produced is the New Jerusalem. We see that all the visions and all the revelations are consummated and manifested in the New Jerusalem. This New Jerusalem is the union and mingling of the processed Triune God with the transformed tripartite man to form one entity as the expression of God in eternity.

I hope that from now on every one of you will be able to speak the same thing. This message is a general outline. Regardless of what subject you cover or what message you speak, never depart from this outline. This is the general subject that must govern your speaking. From now on, this is what we must preach in our gospel preaching; this is what we must teach in our edification of new believers; and this is what we must speak in conferences and trainings. This is the highest gospel, this is what the world needs, and this is what the Lord desires to recover today.

CHAPTER TWO

THE CONSUMMATED SPIRIT

Scripture Reading: Gen. 1:2; Judg. 3:10; Matt. 1:18, 20; 28:19;
2 Cor. 13:14; Col. 1:15, 20; Rom. 6:6; 1 Pet. 1:3; 1 Cor. 15:45b;
2 Cor. 3:17-18; Exo. 30:22-30; 1 John 2:27; Eph. 1:23; Rev. 1:4;
4:5; 5:6; Rom. 8:4, 13; Phil. 1:19

Prayer: Lord, we worship You that You are God, You are
the speaking God, and You are the revealing God. We thank
You from the depths of our being that from the time You
raised up Your recovery in China, You have been speaking to
us and giving us revelation continuously. We truly worship
You today that You have brought us to the high peak of Your
revelation to show us something which most people have not
seen. Through all these years, Lord, You have opened up the
revelation in Your Word. Due to our dullness, however, we
have been very slow in our progress so that after seventy
years the church has just arrived at this situation today. We
truly look to You to enable us to speak this mystery which
cannot be expressed with human words. This is the mystery
of mysteries and the revelation of revelations.

Be with us and anoint us. We trust in Your Spirit. Let us
not only see the light in Your Word but also receive the supply
in Your Spirit. Pour out Your Spirit at this time and anoint us
that You may spontaneously unveil us, illuminate us,
enlighten us, and speak to us—not only to the whole meeting
corporately but also to each one individually. We have a deep
realization that You, our Lord, often meet the needs of many
by the same speaking. O Lord, perform a miracle, a wonder,
again among us right now. Cleanse us with Your precious

blood. By the blood of the Lamb we overcome our accuser daily and stand before our righteous God. Amen.

THE ACCOMPLISHMENT AND APPLICATION OF GOD'S ECONOMY

In this message I have a deep feeling to speak to you a mystery. Actually, I have already spoken to you concerning this mystery in the past thirty years little by little. Some of the items were spoken in one conference and others were spoken in another conference. Some were spoken thirty years ago and others were spoken just last week. The main points of the mystery which I want to fellowship with you were already made known to you and printed in books. In these thirty years I have given thousands of messages, of which forty to fifty were on this mystery, which is the mystery of mysteries, but I did not point it out to you in a thorough way.

What is this mystery concerned with? In the previous message we saw God's eternal economy. Now we need to go on further to see that God's economy needs to be carried out. Any kind of enterprise requires two steps: The first step is to make a product and the next step is to distribute it. When a company plans to manufacture something, first it has to make the product and then it has to promote the sale of the product. One is production, and the other is application. The entire Bible covers God's economy in these two aspects: its accomplishment and its application. The accomplishment of God's economy is a very crucial item, but this time we will not touch it. In this message we need to see how God applies His economy after it has been accomplished.

THE APPLICATION OF GOD'S ECONOMY BEING ALTOGETHER HINGED ON THE SPIRIT

The application of God's economy is altogether hinged on one word—Spirit. The application of God's economy is dependent on the Spirit. In the Bible, the Spirit first refers to the Spirit of God (Gen. 1:2). Afterwards the Bible shows us that the Spirit of God is the Spirit of Jehovah (Judg. 3:10). Then the New Testament goes on to show us that the Spirit of God, the Spirit of Jehovah, is the Holy Spirit (Matt. 1:18, 20), the Spirit who is separated from the common things and thereby is sanctified, made holy. This matter is very deep. "Holy" refers to God's nature, because God's nature is holiness. When holiness is applied to us, that is God imparting His holy nature into us and thereby making us holy. Without God's element, how can we be made holy? In chemistry, if a certain element is missing, it is not possible to obtain the desired result.

How marvelous it is that the name of God is the Father, the Son, and the Spirit (Matt. 28:19). Such a name, however, is not disclosed in the Old Testament; rather, it is somewhat concealed. For example, 2 Samuel 7:12-14 says that David would have a seed, who would call God "Father" and God would call Him "Son." So you see the Father and the Son were there. In the Old Testament the Spirit was clearly mentioned as "the Spirit of God" and the "Spirit of Jehovah." In the Old Testament the name the Father, the Son, and the Spirit is concealed, unlike in the New Testament, in which this name is referred to in plain words.

THE FATHER, THE SON, AND THE SPIRIT BEING INSEPARABLE FROM GOD'S ECONOMY

After He passed through the processes of incarnation, human living, death, and resurrection, the Lord Jesus sanctified and uplifted His humanity into divinity. Thus, He was begotten to be the firstborn Son of God and became the life-giving Spirit. In His resurrection this life-giving Spirit has regenerated God's chosen ones. After He accomplished these things, He came back to His disciples in His resurrection and spoke to them, saying, "All authority has been given to Me in heaven and on earth. Go therefore and disciple all the nations, baptizing them into the name of the Father and of the Son and of the Holy Spirit" (Matt. 28:18-19). It was not until this time that the Father, the Son, and the Spirit were referred to with plain words. The way the Lord Jesus spoke this word and the time, the place, and the situation of His speaking show that the Father, the Son, and the Spirit are very much related to God's economy. Without the Father, the Son, and the Spirit, there would be no possibility for God's economy to be accomplished or applied. Without the Father and the Son, how could there be God's economy and how could it be accomplished? Furthermore, without the Spirit, how could God's economy be applied?

The origination, the accomplishment, and the application of the economy of God cannot be separated from the Triune God. God's economy was planned by the Father; hence, its origin, its source, is the Father. God's economy was accomplished by the Son; hence, its accomplishment is with the Son. God's economy is applied by the Spirit; hence, its application is with the Spirit. The Son accomplished what the Father planned, and the Spirit applies what the Son accomplished. Hence, the name of the Father, the Son, and the Spirit is revealed at a particular time according to the need of a particular divine matter.

THE TRIUNE GOD BEING NOT FOR DOCTRINAL UNDERSTANDING BUT FOR OUR EXPERIENCE

The Bible never speaks of the Triune God as an empty doctrine. It refers to the Spirit of God at the restoration of God's creation. At that time the earth was waste and empty, and the Spirit of God was brooding over the surface of the waters (Gen. 1:2). Later, in God's relationship with man, the Spirit of God was called the Spirit of Jehovah. Then, at the time of God's incarnation, there was the need of the Holy Spirit for His flesh to be set apart and sanctified from the common things. Therefore, the Holy Spirit came (Matt. 1:18, 20). After thirty-three and a half years, the Lord Jesus accomplished God's economy through His death and resurrection. However, after the accomplishment of God's economy, there is still the need of application. Therefore, the Lord charged His disciples to go forth and disciple the nations, baptizing them into the name of the Father and of the Son and of the Spirit (28:19). When it was time for the application of God's economy, the Father, the Son, and the Spirit were fully revealed. All this shows us that it was for such a need and on such an occasion that the Triune God was revealed.

Remember that the Triune God is never an empty doctrine and has absolutely nothing to do with vain, theological

doctrines. The Triune God is not for our doctrinal under-
standing or theological study but for Him to be experienced
by us. Second Corinthians 13:14 says, "The grace of the Lord
Jesus Christ and the love of God and the fellowship of the
Holy Spirit be with you all." This shows us that the Triune
God is not a mere doctrine; He is for our experience. We
cannot know the Triune God by doctrine; we can know Him
only by our experience. If you have not experienced regeneration, you can never know that this God touches people that
they may receive Him and be regenerated.

THE SPIRIT BEING THE CONSUMMATION
OF THE TRIUNE GOD

After the revelation of the Triune God—the Father, the
Son, and the Spirit—the Spirit comes to apply. We need to see
that the application of God's economy is altogether by the
Spirit, the last One of the Divine Trinity. Never consider that
the Spirit is of no importance, thinking that as the last One
among the three, He is not the "head" but the "tail." It is not
so! Among the Father, the Son, and the Spirit, there is no dif-
ference between the first and the last. The Spirit as the last
One of the Father, the Son, and the Spirit is the consummation. The Spirit is the consummation of the Triune God. God
is not three; He is one yet three. With whom is the consummation of the three? It is not with the Father, who is the
initiation; it is neither with the Son, who is the course. The
consummation of the Triune God is with the Spirit. The Spirit
is the consummation of the Triune God.

In the New Testament, from Matthew through Revelation,
whenever something concerning God's relationship with
man is mentioned, the Spirit is also mentioned. The source
is the Father, the course is the Son, and the consummation is
the Spirit. Therefore, the Spirit is the consummation of the
Triune God. Then why is it that before the resurrection of
Christ the name of the Father, the Son, and the Spirit was not
revealed? It is because the economy of God was not yet accomplished. Before Christ's resurrection, the economy of God was
merely a plan; it was not yet accomplished. After Christ came
and accomplished God's economy through His death and

resurrection, it was time for the application; therefore, the Father, the Son, and the Spirit are mentioned. The plan is the commencement, the accomplishment is the process, and the application is the consummation. The consummation is with whom? Not with the Father, nor with the Son, but with the Spirit. This does not mean, however, that since the consummation is with the Spirit, it has nothing to do with the Son or the Father. Because the Son is the embodiment of the Father, and the Spirit is the realization of the Son, the Spirit as the consummation includes the Son as well as the Father. In mathematics, 25 plus 15 plus 30 equals 70; 70 as the sum includes 25, 15, and 30. Likewise, the consummating Spirit includes the Father, the Son, and the Spirit; the Father, the Son, and the Spirit are all consummated in the Spirit.

THE CONSUMMATION OF THE SPIRIT

We need to take a deeper look at the consummated Spirit. This is the main point that I want to fellowship in this message. Genesis 1 refers to the Spirit of God, but that was not the consummated Spirit; the Spirit of Jehovah and the Holy Spirit were not the consummated Spirit either. It was after the resurrection of Christ that the consummated Spirit of the Father, the Son, and the Spirit were revealed. This Spirit is different from the Spirit of God in Genesis, the Spirit of Jehovah in the Old Testament, and the Holy Spirit in Matthew 1. This Spirit is the consummated Spirit. God's economy has been accomplished, and now it needs to be applied. The application is with the consummated Spirit— not merely the aggregate Spirit but the ultimately consummated Spirit.

Now we want to see how the consummated Spirit was completed by being processed. First, we must see that the Spirit of God in Genesis 1 did not have humanity, neither did the Spirit of Jehovah nor the Holy Spirit in Matthew 1. The Holy Spirit in Matthew 1 only brought divinity into humanity, but humanity had not yet entered into divinity. Hence, the Holy Spirit did not have the human element.

Very few people in Christianity today have seen that God possesses humanity. Most people consider that this kind of teaching can lead to heresy. They reason that since God is God, how could He possess humanity? However, we have seen that this is a tremendous revelation in the Bible. From the Spirit of God and the Spirit of Jehovah in the Old Testament to the Holy Spirit at the beginning of the New Testament, God was merely God, and there was no humanity in divinity. Then how was humanity wrought into divinity? This required God to first become a man to bring divinity into humanity and to be joined with humanity. He Himself became a man and lived on this earth for thirty-three and a half years during which time He fully and clearly expressed God by the Holy Spirit. After He fully expressed God, He went to the cross and ended the old creation through His death (Col. 1:15, 20; Rom. 6:6). Then He was raised from the dead, and in His resurrection He fully brought forth the new creation. In this resurrection He first sanctified, uplifted, His humanity and brought it into divinity; thus, He was begotten to be the firstborn Son of God. At the same time, through His resurrection all the God-chosen people of the old creation were regenerated (1 Pet. 1:3); moreover, He became the life-giving Spirit (1 Cor. 15:45b).

Christ's becoming the life-giving Spirit is a tremendous "becoming." The Spirit of God became the consummated Spirit by passing through the processes of incarnation, human living, death, and resurrection. He first put on humanity and then in His resurrection brought humanity into divinity; out of this came the life-giving Spirit. This life-giving Spirit went through all these processes. Without the processes of incarnation, human living, death, and resurrection, the Spirit of God would have remained merely the Spirit of God without any change. The Spirit of God became the life-giving Spirit by passing through the various processes with the various elements added. Therefore, the word *became* involves a great deal. I hope that in the Lord's recovery all these revelations can be released clearly.

Very few in Christianity today have seen this matter; rather, some do not fully believe in what 1 Corinthians 15:45b says: "The last Adam became a life-giving Spirit." This, however, is a word in the Bible which we have to believe. Thank the Lord that He has clearly revealed all these points, one by one, to us all these years. Today the life-giving Spirit is the consummated Spirit. Hence, John 7:39 says that the Spirit was not yet, because Jesus had not yet been glorified in resurrection. Obviously the Holy Spirit was there, and the Spirit of God also was there in Genesis 1, so how could it be that the Spirit was not yet? This is because at that time there was only the old creation without the new creation yet, for Christ was not yet resurrected. Then, at the commencement of the new creation in the resurrection of Christ, the Spirit came into being. That which was originally the Spirit of God has become the Spirit in the resurrection of Christ. This is referred to in 2 Corinthians 3:17: "The Lord is the Spirit." The Spirit, who is revealed to us in 2 Corinthians 3, is carrying out the work of transformation in the believers. We are being transformed because we have the Lord as the Spirit within us. This is why 2 Corinthians 3:18 says that we are being transformed into the same image as the Lord, even as from the Lord Spirit.

THE SPIRIT BEING ALSO THE COMPOUND SPIRIT

Exodus 30 is a record concerning the building of the tabernacle, but in verses 22-30 God suddenly charged Moses to make the holy anointing oil. The way was to take one hin of olive oil and compound it together with four spices; thus, the oil became an ointment. There was one hin of olive oil—the number "one" denotes God, referring to the element of divinity. There were four spices—the number "four" denotes man, referring to the element of humanity. Hence, the mingling of these two is divinity plus humanity. Furthermore, humanity involves four items: myrrh, cinnamon, calamus, and cassia. In brief, myrrh signifies the precious death of Christ; fragrant cinnamon signifies the sweetness and effectiveness of Christ's death; calamus, which is a reed that grows in a marsh or muddy place and is able to shoot up into the air, signifies the precious and transcendent resurrection of Christ; and cassia signifies the power and the effectiveness of Christ's resurrection.

In this holy anointing oil, the aspect of divinity is not as involved as the aspect of humanity. Why? Because Christ came to be a man, and, as a man, He died and resurrected. His death produced an effect, and so did His resurrection. The holy anointing oil with four ingredients indicates that Christ has four elements: He died, and therefore there was the effectiveness of His death; He resurrected, and therefore there was the power of His resurrection. These are four elements. Hence, in the mingling of divinity with humanity, humanity also has these four elements. The holy anointing oil as a type clearly portrays that the Spirit today has divinity, humanity, death with its effectiveness, and resurrection with its power. All these items were compounded together to become the holy anointing oil. In the New Testament, 1 John 2:27 says that we have received the anointing from the Lord; this anointing is the compound Spirit typified by the holy anointing oil.

THE APPLICATION OF GOD'S ECONOMY
BY THE COMPOUND SPIRIT

After Christ accomplished God's economy, the compound Spirit applies it to the people chosen by God. How does He do it? He comes to be mingled with us. He as the compound and consummated Spirit contains the elements of divinity, humanity, death, the effectiveness of His death, resurrection, and the power of His resurrection. When this Spirit comes into us, God comes in, Christ as a person comes in, His death with its effectiveness comes in, and His resurrection with its power comes in. This is an all-inclusive dose that consists of the supply of God, the supply of Christ, the problem-solving and killing effect of Christ's death, and Christ's resurrection with its power. According to the Hebrew language, this is the power to guard against and repel the poison of insects and snakes. In the dwellings of the Jews in ancient times, people were often hurt by snakes and insects. Therefore, they put some cassia in their houses for their own protection. Cassia emits an odor that repels snakes, centipedes, and scorpions. This indicates that the resurrection power of Christ can repel Satan, the evil spirits, and demons.

THE SPIRIT BEING MINGLED WITH US TO BRING FORTH THE CHURCH AND BECOMING THE SEVEN SPIRITS TO MEET THE CHURCH'S NEEDS

Today all that is in the consummated Spirit has been received by us. Because of this, the Spirit has brought forth the church, which is the Body of Christ (Eph. 1:22b-23). The Body of Christ and the Spirit are inseparable. Ephesians 4:4 says, "One Body and one Spirit." Here the Body and the Spirit are joined together. The Spirit brought forth the church, but soon after that, the church became degraded. Hence, the Spirit became the seven Spirits to meet the needs of the degraded church (Rev. 1:4; 4:5; 5:6). This is what the entire book of Revelation shows us.

God is one, but He is also three—the Father, the Son, and the Spirit. The Father planned, the Son came to accomplish what the Father planned, and in the Son's accomplishment the life-giving Spirit was brought forth. This Spirit, who is the transfigured Christ in resurrection, is the consummation of the Triune God. In the degradation of the church, this consummated Spirit became the seven Spirits. God is one yet three, and the three consummated in the life-giving Spirit in resurrection. These three became the one consummated Spirit in the resurrection of Christ. This consummated Spirit became the seven Spirits to meet the needs of the church. God is one yet three, the three are one in resurrection, and then one became seven, the seven Spirits, for the church's need. The seven Spirits are not seven separate Spirits; They denote the sevenfold intensified Spirit. The one Spirit has become the sevenfold intensified Spirit.

BEING IN THE SEVEN SPIRITS BY LIVING AND WALKING ACCORDING TO THE SPIRIT

Where are we living today? Hallelujah! We do not live only in the one Spirit, nor do we live merely in the Triune God. We live in the seven Spirits. In the seven Spirits there are God, man, the death of Christ with its effectiveness, and the resurrection of Christ with its power. Hence, the New Testament tells us that we should live and walk not only in the Spirit but also according to the spirit (Rom. 8:4). The Spirit includes

God, man, Christ's death with its effectiveness, and Christ's resurrection with its power. When you follow this Spirit and walk according to this spirit, all the negative things in you are killed. Therefore, Romans 8:13 says that by the Spirit we should put to death the practices of the body. We ourselves cannot die; we die by receiving the Spirit as the ointment for anointing. The ointment applies the effectiveness of Christ's death to us to produce an effect in us. Today when we use medicated ointment, it kills the germs in us. At the same time, there is the supply in the Spirit as the anointing ointment. Hence, Philippians 1:19 says that this Spirit, the Spirit of Jesus Christ, has the bountiful supply. The negative aspect is the problem-solving by killing, and the positive aspect is the bountiful supply. Both aspects are in the consummated Spirit.

A CLOSING PRAYER

Lord, we worship You that You are such a God; You are the consummated Spirit to be the God whom we worship. You are not the same as the God in Judaism; You are also different from the God in Mohammedanism. You are such a processed and consummated Spirit. You are one God, yet You are also three; in resurrection You are one in becoming the consummated Spirit; and for the need of the church You have become the sevenfold intensified Spirit. We truly worship You and thank You. In creation You are the Spirit of God; in God's relationship with man You are the Spirit of Jehovah; in God's incarnation You are the Holy Spirit; for the bringing forth of the church, You, as the Holy Spirit, became the life-giving, consummated Spirit; and for the needs of the church, You, as the life-giving Spirit, became the sevenfold intensified Spirit. Today we are in this Spirit. This is our Lord, this is our God, this is our Redeemer, this is our Savior, and this is our Master, the One whom we serve. We truly desire to live in You as such a God, that is, to live in the Spirit, according to Your heart's desire.

CHAPTER THREE

THE REALITY OF THE BODY OF CHRIST

Scripture Reading: Eph. 1:22-23; 1 Cor. 12:12; Col. 3:10-11; Rev. 21:1; 2 Pet. 3:10-12; Rom. 6:6; Gal. 2:20-21; Eph. 2:5; Rom. 1:3-4; John 1:18; Rom. 8:3; Acts 13:33; Rom. 8:29; 2 Cor. 5:21; Heb. 4:15; Phil. 3:10

AN ADDITIONAL WORD TO THE PREVIOUS MESSAGE ON THE CONSUMMATED SPIRIT

The previous message on the consummated Spirit may be summarized as follows: God is triune; He became a man and passed through death and resurrection; in resurrection the Triune God—the Father, the Son, and the Spirit—has a consummation, and this consummation is the life-giving Spirit. This life-giving Spirit is the consummation of the processes through which the Triune God passed; in this consummated Spirit the church was brought forth. Then the church became degraded, and the life-giving Spirit as the consummation of the Triune God became the seven Spirits, the sevenfold intensified Spirit.

Throughout the generations theologians have discussed the truth concerning the Divine Trinity and the person of Christ; this discussion began as early as the second century with the church fathers. Although what they saw concerning the Divine Trinity was clear, it was not as deep as what we see today. They also saw something concerning the person of Christ—that He is both God and man. Furthermore, they saw that God became man that man might become God. However, later theologians retained only the first two points, the

Divine Trinity of God and the divinity and humanity of Christ, which have been taught until the present time. The third point, which is concerning God becoming man for man to become God, has rarely been referred to.

CHRIST BEING THE HEAD AND THE BODY

My burden in this message is for us to see the reality of the Body of Christ. Ephesians 1:22-23 shows us that Christ is the Head and the church is His Body. But 1 Corinthians 12:12 says, "For even as the body is one and has many members, yet all the members of the body, being many, are one body, so also is the Christ." According to this verse, Christ is not only the Head but also the Body with all the members. Thus, Christ is the Head and Christ is also the Body. Both the Head and the Body are Christ.

Furthermore, Colossians 3:10-11 shows us that in the new man, that is, in the new creation, the church, there cannot be Greek and Jew, circumcision and uncircumcision, barbarian, Scythian, slave, free man, but Christ is all and in all. Christ is all the members of the new man and in all the members of the new man.

Some may ask, "There is no problem in saying that Christ is the Head. But if we say that Christ is the Body, then how about us? Didn't we say that the believers are the members of the Body of Christ? If the Body is also Christ, what about the believers?" How do we answer this question?

THE BODY OF CHRIST BEING GOD'S NEW CREATION

The answer is this: The Body of Christ is God's new creation. According to biblical principles, the new creation of God comes out of His old creation. God's old creation was something created out of nothing, but it is not so with God's new creation. God's new creation comes out of the existing old things. For example, the new heaven and the new earth spoken of at the end of the Bible are not something out of nothing; they are produced out of the old heaven and the old earth. On the one hand, Revelation 21:1 shows us that the new heaven and the new earth will appear after the passing away of the first heaven and the first earth. On the other hand, 2 Peter 3:10-12 shows us that when that day comes, the heavens, the earth, and all the elements will be dissolved by burning fire. After the burning, the old heavens and old earth will be renewed into the new heavens and new earth.

The Bible says that we have been crucified with Christ (Gal. 2:20). In particular, Romans says clearly that our old man has been crucified with Christ (6:6). But this is not all. Not only have we died with Christ, but we have also been resurrected with Christ. Hence, Ephesians 2:5 says that God made us alive together with Christ. Therefore, when a person is buried through baptism, he is finished and it is no longer he; but this does not mean that he remains buried in the water without rising again. He is not only immersed, buried, in the water, but subsequently he rises out of the water. This signifies death and resurrection. What is buried is the man of the old creation; what is resurrected is the man of the new creation. The old creation was created out of nothing, but it is not so with the new creation. The new creation is produced out of the old creation through death and resurrection. When Paul said, "I am crucified with Christ," that "I" was Paul as an old creation. Hence, it was no longer Paul as an old creation who lived; it was Paul as a new creation who lived.

THE BODY OF CHRIST BEING PRODUCED
THROUGH DEATH AND RESURRECTION

In the Body of Christ, the Head is uniquely Christ, and the Body is produced by the God-chosen people passing through Christ's death and resurrection. In the old creation we died and were buried with Christ completely. However, in the resurrection power of Christ we were resurrected. The original creation came out of God; it was something created by God and it was good. But later it was poisoned by Satan. Satan's poison entered into the man originally created by God so that, in addition to the original element created by God, other elements were added; these elements are death, the world, sin, the flesh, and Satan. Hence, God's original creation became old, and its nature was changed, having things other than that created by God.

Therefore, when Christ brought us with Him in His death on the cross, He brought the entire old creation with Him to die there. In His resurrection He was raised with the part which was created by God. "No longer I" means that it is no longer the fallen "I" in the old creation. "I now live" refers to the resurrected "I" in the new creation. This resurrected "I" is joined with Christ as one. How did Christ resurrect us? In His resurrection He mingled His divinity with our humanity; thus, we were resurrected. Hence, we can either say that the Body of Christ is Christ, or we can say that the Body of Christ is all the members of the Body of Christ.

THE HUMAN PART OF CHRIST BEING DESIGNATED THE SON OF GOD BY THE SPIRIT OF HOLINESS THROUGH DEATH AND RESURRECTION

Romans 1:3-4 says, "Concerning His Son, who came out of the seed of David according to the flesh, who was designated the Son of God in power according to the Spirit of holiness out of the resurrection of the dead, Jesus Christ our Lord." Christ is not only man but also God. His divine part is the Spirit, that is, God Himself, the Spirit of holiness. When Christ died, His entire being was hung on the cross. However, because He had the Spirit of holiness within Him, that Spirit enlivened Him out of death and designated Him the Son of God.

Before His incarnation Christ already was the Son of God (John 1:18; Rom. 8:3). By incarnation He put on an element, the human flesh, which had nothing to do with divinity; that part of Him needed to be sanctified and uplifted by passing through death and resurrection. By resurrection His human nature was sanctified, uplifted, and transformed. Hence, by resurrection He, with His humanity, was designated the Son of God, that is, the firstborn Son of God.

If Christ was only man and not God, when He died and was buried, He would have been finished. But He was man and God. Although His human part died, His divine part, which could not die, lives forever. Christ could be resurrected from the dead because He has the divine element in Him, and that divine element is the Spirit of holiness. This Spirit of holiness was able to resurrect Him out of death and designate

Him the Son of God. By this designation His humanity was uplifted into divinity and was joined with divinity to be one. Consequently, He was completely the Son of God. When He lived in the flesh, a part of Him was merely man, merely the seed of David; that part was not the Son of God. How did that part become the Son of God? It was by the designation through death and resurrection.

Acts 13:33 says, "You are My Son; today I have begotten You." Here "today" refers to the day of Christ's resurrection. Christ was begotten in His resurrection to be the firstborn Son of God. In resurrection the human part of Christ was made alive by God and uplifted into divinity. In this way Christ was begotten to be the firstborn Son of God (Rom. 8:29).

Since Christ is the firstborn Son of God, we as the many sons of God are exactly the same as He. However, because His humanity was without sin and had never become fallen (2 Cor. 5:21; Heb. 4:15), His human part did not need to be redeemed but it needed to be uplifted. Our humanity consists of two parts: one part is the God-created part, and the other part is the fallen and corrupted part. When Christ brought us with Him to die on the cross, our fallen, corrupted part died and ended together with Him, but the God-created part within us was made alive together with Him by the power which raised Him from the dead (Eph. 2:5).

Today Christ is the union and mingling of God with man. Likewise, we are the union and mingling of God with man and man with God. This is the Body of Christ. This is the normal believer's living, which is not merely God's living or man's living; it is a God-man living. This is just like when the Lord was on this earth. His living was not merely God's living or man's living; it was a living that lived out God in humanity.

THE REALITY OF THE BODY OF CHRIST—
THE GOD-MAN LIVING

God's salvation is altogether not a matter of religious improvement or a matter of moral and ethical improvement. God's salvation is to put us into the death of Christ and then to bring us out of that death. Christ's being put into death was something done by the Jews together with the Roman soldiers. However, Christ's resurrection from death was something carried out not by man but by the Spirit of holiness in Him. Today it is the same with us. When we were baptized, we were immersed into the water by men. If we did not have the Spirit of God within us, our rising out of the water would be in vain, having no reality of resurrection. But we have the Spirit in us, so we have the reality of resurrection. This is true with all believers. When they live in a corporate way, what they live out is the Body of Christ. This is absolutely different from the teachings of Confucius and the teachings of religion. All the ethical teachings of Confucius and all the doctrines of religion come out of the tree of the knowledge of good and evil instead of the tree of life. God's salvation brings us into death and then brings us out of death. It not only redeems us but also uplifts us that we may enter into divinity and live in God, that is, in life. We live by and according to this life; we do not walk according to good and evil. It is in this way that we have the reality of the Body of Christ.

Is the Lord's recovery the Body of Christ? It depends on whether or not the believers are living the God-man life. Therefore, we must see that teaching people merely according to the letter of Scriptures is not the Body of Christ; that is a religious work. Merely using the words in the Bible to teach people to flee evil and do good is equivalent to the teachings of Confucius; this does not result in the Body of Christ. Even we may preach the gospel zealously, but unless our gospel preaching is the issue of a God-man living, it is not the Body of Christ. What is the Body of Christ? The Body of Christ is a group of God-chosen people who have been redeemed and regenerated through death and resurrection. They have been united and mingled with God and have been living in this union all the time since their regeneration. In such a union they are sanctified, renewed, transformed, conformed, and, eventually, glorified.

If we live such a life, we are the Body of Christ. If we do not live such a life, what we have is just something similar to the ethical teachings of Confucius and the superficial activities of religion. Hence, in our preaching the gospel, expounding the Bible, or visiting the brothers and sisters, we should check whether it is something lived out of a God-man living. Only that which is lived out of a God-man living is the Body of Christ. Otherwise, it is just a religious activity in society, which is no different from the moral teachings of Confucius; it belongs to the tree of the knowledge of good and evil instead of the tree of life.

THE REALITY OF THE BODY OF CHRIST— A LIVING OF BEING CONFORMED TO THE DEATH OF CHRIST THROUGH THE CROSS

This God-man living is also a living of being conformed to the death of Christ through the cross. This conformation to the death of Christ is through the power of Christ's resurrection (Phil. 3:10). We must be those who live a crucified life continually by taking Christ's death as the mold of our life. It is only by living this kind of life that we can have the reality of the Body of Christ. May the Lord have mercy on us so that we can live a life of being conformed to the death of Christ through the cross. May the Lord open our eyes to see this vision. Only those who have passed through death and resurrection can have their eyes opened; they live and walk by the revelation which they have seen. Only such a living is the God-man living, and only such a living can live out the reality of the Body of Christ.

CHAPTER FOUR

THE PROPER LIVING
OF A CHRIST-PURSUING GOD-MAN

Scripture Reading: Phil. 3:10; 1:19-21; 4:13; Rom. 8:4; Phil. 4:12

OUTLINE

I. Pursuing to know Christ—Phil. 3:10a.

II. Pursuing to know the power of Christ's resurrection—Phil. 3:10b.

III. Pursuing to live a life of dying with Christ to be conformed to His death by the power of His resurrection—Phil. 3:10c.

IV. Living Christ to magnify Him through the bountiful supply of the Spirit of Jesus Christ—Phil. 1:19-21a.

V. Living and walking in the empowering Christ—Phil. 4:13.

VI. Living and walking in and according to the mingled spirit—Rom. 8:4.

VII. In everything taking Christ as the secret—Phil. 4:12. This being:

   A. To live out the processed and consummated Triune God.

   B. To live out the pneumatic Christ as the embodiment of the Triune God.

   C. To live out the consummated Spirit as the consummation of the processed Triune God.

   D. This being equivalent to living in the resurrection (denoting a person) of the consummated Spirit.

This also being:

A. To live out the reality of the Body of Christ.

B. To become an unprecedented revival among all the Christ-pursuing God-men today.

C. To be the means for the Lord to close this age and bring in His kingdom age.

If God thru th' Eternal Spirit
Nail me ever with the Lord;
Only then as death is working
Will His life thru me be poured.

This kind of living requires our pursuit. A God-man is one who lives under the cross daily. Hence, to have merely the teaching of the cross is not enough; the cross must become our experience.

Such a living in the shadow of the cross touches the deepest part of our being and every detail in our life. We all know that we need to be careful when we talk to others. We brothers who are married, however, realize that we become very careless when we are talking to our wife. If we are those who live in the shadow of the cross, even our talking to our wife needs to be checked. Are we under the death of the cross when we talk to our wife in a certain way? If we are willing to check in this way, we will see that ninety-nine percent of the things which we say to our wife should never be said. They are things which we speak out of ourself; they are not spoken by the indwelling God in us, but by our natural man. It may be that we do not criticize, judge, or condemn others; instead, we speak nice things about others. But is it Christ who speaks, or is it we who speak? We have to admit that most of the things we say are by ourself without passing through the cross.

If this can be practiced among us, all troubles will disappear. This not only means that we should not engage in gossip, speaking idle words, but also means that we should not even speak nice words, because we are those who need to die and be in the shadow of the cross. We should not speak but allow the Lord to speak. If we truly have this experience, regardless of what we say, we have the cross checking in us: "Is this spoken through the cross? Is the mold of the cross here?"

The principle is the same in our shopping. We all like to buy things. It is not a matter of whether we should buy a certain item but a matter of the cross. Even in small matters such as buying a necktie we need to be in the shadow of the cross. We are those who belong to Christ; in other words, we are God-men. Therefore, we should live under the death of the cross in all things. It is in this way that the resurrected Lord can manifest His power from within us.

LIVING CHRIST TO MAGNIFY HIM THROUGH THE BOUNTIFUL SUPPLY OF THE SPIRIT OF JESUS CHRIST

The proper life of a Christ-pursuing God-man is also a life of living Christ to magnify Him through the bountiful supply of the Spirit of Jesus Christ. We must not only know the power of Christ's resurrection and be conformed to His death daily, but we must also know the bountiful supply of the Spirit of Jesus Christ. By this bountiful supply we can live Christ to magnify Him (Phil. 1:19-21a). Paul wrote this word during his imprisonment in Rome. Under that difficult circumstance he wrote that by the bountiful supply of the Spirit of Jesus Christ, he was enabled to live and magnify Christ. When he was to be martyred, knowing that he was going to be with the Lord, he wrote in the second Epistle to Timothy, "I have fought the good fight; I have finished the course; I have kept the faith. Henceforth there is laid up for me the crown of righteousness" (4:7-8a). Hence, he rejoiced. Under that condition and situation he overcame the threatening of death and martyrdom and lived out Christ to magnify Him. Paul was able to live out that kind of life because he did it by the bountiful supply of the Spirit of Jesus Christ.

We do not yet have adequate experience of the bountiful supply of the Spirit of Jesus Christ. Hence, we need to pursue. Since we are God-men, we should live out God. God's desire is that we become Him through the bountiful supply of the Spirit of Jesus Christ so that we can die to ourselves and Christ can live out of us and be magnified through us.

LIVING AND WALKING IN THE EMPOWERING CHRIST

The proper life of a God-man who pursues Christ is to live and walk in the empowering Christ (Phil. 4:13).

LIVING AND WALKING
IN AND ACCORDING TO THE MINGLED SPIRIT

Furthermore, we should live and walk in and according to the mingled spirit (Rom. 8:4). Paul said that we are approved and justified before God because we live, walk, and have our being according to the mingled spirit. A person who walks according to the mingled spirit is one who lives and walks in the empowering Christ.

IN EVERYTHING TAKING CHRIST AS THE SECRET

A Christ-pursuing God-man should live by taking Christ as the secret in everything (Phil. 4:12). This is a very deep pursuit and experience. What is a secret? A secret is the key or skillfulness to do something. This is just like a key being the secret to a lock. Without the key we cannot open the lock; to open the lock we must have the key. In accomplishing anything we must have the secret; otherwise, we will waste our effort. Paul did everything by taking Christ as his key to open his "locks."

THE ISSUE OF LIVING
ACCORDING TO THE ABOVE SEVEN ITEMS

If we engage in the above pursuits, the issue will be that we live out the processed and consummated Triune God. We live out not only the Father and the Son but also the Spirit. Furthermore, we live out the pneumatic Christ as the embodiment of the Triune God. Christ is the embodiment of the Triune God; He is also the Spirit Himself. Christ Himself is the Spirit and the Triune God.

We also live out the consummated Spirit of the processed Triune God. Christ passed through resurrection to become the life-giving Spirit; this Spirit is the consummation of the processed Triune God. Hence, the Spirit, the life-giving Spirit, is the consummation of the Triune God, and Christ is the very Spirit. If we live a life according to the preceding seven items, we live out not only the Triune God and Christ but also the consummated Spirit.

When we thus live out the consummated Spirit, this is equivalent to living in the resurrection of the consummated

Spirit. This resurrection denotes a person, not a power or a thing. This is why the Lord Jesus said that He is the resurrection (John 11:25). Furthermore, the reality of resurrection is the Spirit, the consummation of the Triune God. Therefore, we have this conclusion: The Triune God, Christ, the Spirit, and resurrection are one. When we live according to the preceding seven items, we live in resurrection. This resurrection denotes a person—God. Hence, to be in resurrection means to be in the Triune God, in Christ, and in the consummated Spirit.

TO LIVE OUT THE REALITY OF THE BODY OF CHRIST

As the new creation, we should not live in the old creation. If we live in the old creation, we are not in resurrection but in our natural man. Once we live in the Triune God, in Christ, and in the consummated Spirit, we are in resurrection. This is a life that lives out the reality of the Body of Christ. Today, in general, people have the term "the Body of Christ," yet very few know what the Body of Christ refers to. The Brethren teaching says that the church is the Body of Christ. This is literally according to Ephesians 1:23: "Which [the church] is His Body, the fullness of the One who fills all in all." But what is the Body of Christ? The Brethren did not have a clear explanation.

Based on his knowledge of the Bible and his own experience, Brother Watchman Nee spoke a word which probably had never been spoken by anyone else. He said, "The Spirit is the reality of resurrection." When we live in this resurrection, what we live out is the Body of Christ. The Body of Christ is the issue of the God-man life lived out by all those who believe in and belong to the Lord as the new man. Only such a God-man living is Christ. In our daily life we should speak and do things in resurrection. If we are not in resurrection, we are not the Body of Christ; rather, we are natural. We may live and walk in a proper manner, but if we do not live out the reality of Christ, we are not in the Spirit or in the reality of resurrection; hence, we are without the reality of the Body of Christ. This touches something very high. If we have not seen this, we have not seen the Body of Christ.

CHAPTER FIVE

THE BODY OF CHRIST AND THE CHURCH

Scripture Reading: Rom. 12:4-5; 1 Cor. 12:12-27; Eph. 1:22-23; 4:4; Col. 1:18; 2:19; 3:15; 1 Tim. 3:15-16

Prayer: O Lord, we still look to You for Your leading. We really have nothing and can do nothing. Apart from You we are nothing. Lord, we truly need You. We pray that You would save us from speaking any unnecessary words and give us fresh words with fresh light, fresh vision, and fresh supply. We worship You from the depths of our being that You are and we are not; You are everything and we are nothing. Hence, we are here in the place of death looking to You that we may live in resurrection. Cleanse us with Your precious blood and resist the enemy's attack for us. Lord, You know Your enemy; we accuse him before You. All our hardships are from him. O Lord, rebuke him on our behalf. Destroy him for us in these days of warfare. He was already destroyed on the cross; we ask You to destroy his power of darkness and all the unclean spirits and demons. Draw a line around Your recovery with Your blood so that the enemy, Satan, cannot go even one step beyond the line which You have fixed. We realize that You have given us lessons for us to learn. Nevertheless, we ask You not to allow Your enemy to exceed the limit; rather, restrict him. Under Your precious blood we tell him, "May the Lord rebuke you, and may He restrict you!" Amen.

My burden in this message is for us to see the Body of Christ and the church. We are too familiar with these two terms. But what is the Body of Christ? What is the church? Very few can answer accurately. Therefore, we need to ask ourselves what the Body of Christ actually is and what the church actually is.

THE BODY OF CHRIST

In the Bible the Body of Christ is referred to only in the Epistles of Paul; it is not even mentioned by the Lord Jesus in the Gospels. Furthermore, only four of the fourteen Epistles written by Paul speak concerning the Body of Christ: Romans mentions it only in one place; 1 Corinthians deals with it to a great extent; Ephesians covers it to a lesser extent; and Colossians is the last book dealing with it. Hence, if we desire to know the Body of Christ, we must have a thorough study of these four Epistles.

Because so many things are covered in these four Epistles, the readers of the Bible are easily distracted by them. Suppose you go to a jewelry store to buy something. If too many items are on display, your eyes are dazzled. Hence, all the salespersons have been trained to show the customers only one item at a time instead of showing many items all at once. The biggest problem with us who read the Bible is that we are often distracted by the great number of items dealt with in the Bible. Therefore, when we study the Bible, we must learn one thing—we should grasp the main points of the Bible and not be distracted by many other items.

In Romans

In Romans, Paul mentions the Body of Christ only in one place, and that is in 12:4-5, which says, "For just as in one body we have many members, and all the members do not have the same function, so we who are many are one body in Christ, and individually members one of another." This is the only place you can find in Romans that mentions the Body of Christ. When Bible readers come to Romans, it is very difficult for them not to be distracted by the other things. You must grasp the main points of Romans, study the book slowly to familiarize yourself with it, and have a thorough knowledge of the intrinsic significance of the book. Then you will see that among all the main points and items in Romans, the most important thing is the Body of Christ. We say that God

If we practice exercising our spirit in our daily life, spontaneously we will exercise our spirit as soon as we get into the meetings; we will not have a set form, nor will we need to be directed by someone to do certain things. When we come to the meetings, there should not be any set of rules or any definite arrangement. Before coming to the meeting hall, even while at home you may begin the meeting by exercising your spirit to pray, "Lord, I praise You; remember and bless the meeting today." After you get into your car, you and your wife with your children—the four of you—are already having a meeting. Once you enter through the gate of the meeting hall, you say, "Praise the Lord, hallelujah, I can come in through the gate of Zion." When you go up the stairs, you can sing one of the Songs of Ascents, praying and praising step by step. This way of coming to the meetings is the overflow of the exercise of our spirit in our practical living.

Any ritualistic practice is not the church. The church depends on life and spirit. The church meetings should be living and freed from rituals and forms. However, to this day we do not have this practice because we are not living and do not exercise our spirit. This is similar to what the Lord said to the church in Sardis: "You have a name that you are living, and yet you are dead." In the Lord's eyes Christians today are living in name but dead in reality. All genuine Christians should be living and full of the Spirit. If you are living and full of the Spirit, you will preach the gospel to those whom you meet. But how many today have such a living practice? I hope that henceforth you will overturn all the dead rituals. We say that we need to have the God-man living. How can God-men not have the life of God? And how can God-men not have the Spirit of God? We are God-men, not dead men. God-men should be living and full of the Spirit.

THE REALITY OF THE HOUSE OF GOD
BEING THE REALITY OF THE BODY OF CHRIST

In the Bible the most thorough and the highest speaking concerning the house of God is in 1 Timothy 3:15-16, which says, "But if I delay, I write that you may know how one ought to conduct himself in the house of God, which is the church of the living God, the pillar and base of the truth. And confessedly, great is the mystery of godliness: He who was manifested in the flesh, / Justified in the Spirit, / Seen by angels, / Preached among the nations, / Believed on in the world, / Taken up in glory." All orthodox students of the Bible acknowledge that the emphasis of verse 16 is not on Christ but on the church. The church is the great mystery of godliness, the manifestation of God in the flesh, and the pillar and base of the truth. The pillar supports the building, and the base holds the pillar. The church as such a pillar and base bears and holds the truth of God. The truth here refers to the real things revealed in the New Testament concerning Christ and the church according to God's New Testament economy. The church is the supporting pillar and holding base of all the realities.

Since the church is the house of the living God, it is a matter of life and spirit. Both the Body of Christ and the house of God are organic; both are hinged on the life of God and the Spirit of God. Without the life of God or the Spirit of God, both the house of God and the Body of Christ are gone. All that is left is a human organization, a mere assembling of the called-out congregation. If there is no life or spirit, there is no reality of the Body of Christ. Moreover, if there is no life or spirit, there is no reality of the house of God.

In the previous message I said that the proper living of a Christ-pursuing God-man is to live out the reality of the Body of Christ. In this message I would like to add something more: A God-man should also live out the reality of the house of God. Actually, the reality of the house of God is the reality of the Body of Christ. The house of God is local; the Body of Christ is universal. Both are the same in their intrinsic essence; both depend on life and spirit.

To the church in Sardis the Lord said, "You have a name that you are living, and yet you are dead" (Rev. 3:1). To the church in Laodicea He said, "Because you are lukewarm and neither hot nor cold, I am about to spew you out of My mouth" (v. 16). The degraded church has a name that she is living, and yet she is dead; she is also lukewarm toward the Lord. To such a degraded church Christ is standing outside her door instead of inside (v. 20). This is the general situation of

Christianity today. Christ is outside the door of the so-called church instead of being inside. That it is merely an organization is apparent; it is not the house of God or the Body of Christ. Hence, in reality it cannot be counted as the house of God or the Body of Christ; it has neither the reality of the house of God nor the reality of the Body of Christ. Such a danger exists also among us. When we meet, Christ may be outside instead of being inside.

Today if we want to bring in an unprecedented revival, we must deal with the matter of life and spirit. I hope to see that some of you will really exercise your spirit to be filled with the Spirit regularly. If so, once you step into the meeting hall, you will be singing and praising; you will sing going up the stairs and walking through the aisles, and even when you sit down you will still be singing and praising without ceasing. If we have this kind of meeting among us, this is indeed the manifestation of the Body of Christ, and this is where the house of God is. When people come into our midst, according to what 1 Corinthians 14:25 says, they will worship God, declaring that indeed God is among us.

CHAPTER SIX

THE LORD'S MOVE IN HIS RECOVERY

Scripture Reading: Eph. 4:1-16; 2:11-22; 1 Tim. 3:15-16

Prayer: Lord, we thank You for being with us and blessing us in the past five meetings. We need Your presence and blessing even more in this final meeting. Lord, lead us in this meeting to have fellowship with one another and cause us to open ourselves to You and also to one another without any shadow, covering, or hiding, and even more, without any pretense or hypocrisy. O Lord, give us a pure heart and an open spirit. May You be set free, released, from within us. Enable us to have fellowship with one another, show concern for one another, and bear one another's burden in You as the all-penetrating Spirit.

Lord, remember Your recovery on the earth. We truly thank You that now Your recovery has reached the six continents. Lord, there is the spreading in so many places, especially in Russia, Poland, Romania, Switzerland, even in Germany, and even more in the United Kingdom. For this we worship You. We also look to You for Your supply to meet our needs. We can never forget that we are not, but You are; we have nothing, but You have everything. O Lord, may You exercise Your might, especially in the last days, and grant us an unprecedented revival everywhere that You may be able to close this age and usher in Your kingdom age. All this requires us to cooperate with You by praying to You to touch Your throne and by presenting ourselves more to You. May You bring in more young people to receive the training that we may meet the great need in spreading to different places. Lord, remember us. Amen.

BRINGING IN THE NEW WAY IN TAIWAN SINCE 1984

In this message I would like to fellowship with you concerning the Lord's move in His recovery. In 1984 I went back to Taiwan. Although I did not know what the real reason was, I had a clear burden within me that I had to go back. In Taipei I was led by the Lord to bring up the matter concerning the new way. By 1984 the Lord's recovery had been on the earth for sixty-two years; except for the first ten years, I directly participated in His recovery. Although I did not attend the meetings in those ten years, I had fellowship through correspondence. In 1933 when I left my job and went to Shanghai, I was immediately asked by Brother Nee to stay there as his long-term guest. That visit lasted nearly five months. At that time he did not have that much work to do, so he could afford me a great amount of time. I grasped that rare opportunity to frequently go to him for instruction. He spoke to me concerning the Lord's recovery, item by item, from the beginning; he even told me the two-thousand-year history of the Lord's church on the earth in its entirety. From then on, I have remained in the Lord's recovery.

By 1984 I had been in the Lord's recovery for fifty-two years. At that time, however, I felt very heavy concerning the situation of the Lord's recovery both in the United States and in the Far East, especially in Taipei. The general condition both in the United States and in the Far East had more or less entered into dormancy; it was as if everyone was asleep. That was something incomprehensible to me. At that time I did not know what to do. Therefore, I told the brothers and sisters in America that I needed to take off from my work and leave the United States possibly for one or two years. But this did not mean that I would not come back. I said that I would still come back several times every year. I would come back for the winter and summer trainings and other important conferences; I would come back three or four times every year. I considered that the foundation in the United States had been laid and that the work here was on the right track; hence, the brothers would know how to go on. I could not tell them what I was going to do in Taiwan, but I assured them that whatever was carried out there would be made known to the United States through my fellowship. After such a word of explanation, I went back to Taiwan.

In Taipei, on the one hand, I began to study the new way and hold trainings for it; on the other hand, I began to do the work of the Chinese translation of the Recovery Version of the New Testament. From 1984 to 1985, concerning the Chinese Recovery Version, I found out that I had to be involved personally because no one knew what was within me and no one knew the Bible so deeply or intrinsically. Therefore, I considered that if we would publish the Chinese Version, I had no choice but to labor painstakingly on it. Hence, I labored in Taipei for several years and did not return to the United States until 1989. In Taipei I worked day and night; at night I often worked until eleven o'clock and sometimes even twelve o'clock. In the translation of the text of the Recovery Version, I considered every sentence and decided on every word; I also finalized all the footnotes. The work of the Recovery Version in Chinese was completed in 1989. Then I felt that I had spent enough time in Taiwan and had to return to the United States.

THE OPPOSITION AND REBELLION STIRRED UP BY THE NEW WAY

As soon as I mentioned the new way in Taipei, it stirred up an opposition. The opposition actually began in 1984 but was not manifested until 1987. From 1984, several people began to spread the rumor that Brother Lee's ministry was off and that they would not follow any longer. It seems that those few brothers volunteered themselves to be the heroes in the Lord's recovery with the intention to restore the Lord's recovery. Hence, they began to contact others to join them in overthrowing Brother Lee's ministry. They maintained the attitude that they were the heroes to oppose Brother Lee and restore the Lord's recovery. Therefore, it was not an accidental rebellion or a temporary dissension; rather, there was a long period of fermentation and an overall plan.

In the beginning when I faced that situation, I remained quiet before the Lord, because I was very clear within. I have been walking on this way with Brother Nee, and in these scores of years Brother Nee had laid the foundation. From 1922 to 1952 the Lord's recovery in mainland China was under the leadership of Brother Nee. Later, when the move of the Lord's recovery was restricted on the mainland, I was brought overseas by the Lord. Spontaneously, the leadership came upon my shoulders. Everything that I did was absolutely in the same steps with Brother Nee, not only in the light of the truth but also in the aspect of life. I never departed from whatever Brother Nee did. Gradually, the Lord showed us something deeper and higher. In 1987 when that kind of situation was exposed, I did not say anything because within me I was very clear that no one could change the Lord's recovery which is built upon truth as well as life.

I was very clear concerning what Brother Nee spoke; I also knew very well what I spoke. In 1951 I began to release a publication in Chinese entitled *The Ministry of the Word*. From that time until 1987 I released a great number of messages. At least three thousand messages were given in America and printed into books. When those people began to oppose me, I checked with myself concerning whether I had erred in the truth. Eventually, however, I could not find any mistake in my leadership of the Lord's recovery. The opposers alleged, first, that since 1984 I had changed and departed from the way led by Brother Nee, and second, that I exercised control. Concerning the second point, they strongly condemned me and said some very ugly things about me, such as Brother Lee being a king and a pope. When I heard all these things, I did not say anything. I realized that every step concerning the foundation laid by this recovery on the earth and the building in these sixty to seventy years was accurate; no one can touch or change anything.

THE LORD'S VINDICATION

It has been seven years since the turmoil of 1987. I believe that in these seven years the Lord has clearly vindicated His recovery. This was evidenced in the recent conference in Hong

The training facilities in Anaheim can accommodate a maximum of one hundred fifty people. We need to improve our facilities to accommodate more people for the training.

On the one hand, we need to train people, and on the other hand, we need to spread out, especially to Europe. Those who go to Russia and Europe will still consist mainly of Caucasians, particularly Americans. However, the twenty who went from Taiwan to Russia have also been very much welcomed. Now we have over one hundred co-workers in Russia, three-fourths of whom are Americans; one-fourth are Chinese, and some are co-workers who have been raised up locally in these two to three years. I believe from now on the ratio should be that if there are three hundred going from the United States, one hundred should be going from Taiwan. Such a coordination will be more effective than having only Americans going there. Now many cities in Russia are ready and are just waiting for people to go there. At the beginning of next year, those in the two big cities, Moscow and St. Petersburg, will go out in teams for the spreading. Each team will consist of one Russian (raised up in these few years and able to take the lead), one American, and one Chinese.

I am fellowshipping these things with you so that you brothers can realize that the training in Taiwan needs strengthening. You must pick up the talented ones, those who are college graduates and good in English, and bring them in to be properly trained. After two years of training, they can go forth. Likewise, the training in the United States accepts only those who have graduated from college. It is not as easy to gain people in the United States as it is in Taiwan. However, the United States is bigger than Taiwan. Today in the United States there are over two hundred churches scattered in different places; the work at the universities has also spread. Hence, the number of people attending the full-time training has increased steadily. Once they finish their training, some can go to Russia, and some can go to Poland and other places.

CONCERNING THE LIFE-STUDY TRAININGS

On the personal side now, due to my age, I cannot do too much and much less go to visit faraway places. The life-study trainings will probably be completed by the summer or winter of next year. This winter we will cover 1 and 2 Chronicles, Ezra, Nehemiah, and Esther and thereby conclude the historical books. Next year we will cover Proverbs, Ecclesiastes, and Song of Songs, thereby concluding the life-study trainings on the entire Bible. After that, every winter and summer training, the Lord willing, we will specifically cover the crystallization of the main points. What you have been hearing these days is mostly the crystallized speaking. This means that I will re-study the main points in the New Testament. This is my burden. Of course, at the same time, I will still be here helping the full-time training and also leading the church. All these things require your intercession.

NEEDING TO BE EXERCISED IN SPIRIT AND LIFE

What you need to do now is go back and help the saints in the exercise of the spirit. We need to show the brothers and sisters that without life and spirit, there is no reality of the church, there is no reality of the Body of Christ, and there is no reality of the house of God. Both the Body of Christ and the house of God hinge on life and spirit. You have to repeatedly read and pray-read Ephesians 4:1-16, 2:11-22, and 1 Timothy 3:15-16. These three portions of the Word are on the house, the household of God, and also on the Body of Christ. If you get into the depths of these portions, you will realize that both the house of God and the Body of Christ hinge on life and spirit. Life and spirit are the reality, the substance, of the Body of Christ. The same is true with the house of God. Without life and spirit, the house of God is finished; it is vanity and insubstantial. First Timothy 3:15 says that the house of God is the pillar and base of God's truth. This God is the living God, and the church is the house of the living God. This house is the great mystery of godliness, of God manifested in the flesh. This is the church.

A local church must be in a condition that is full of life and spirit, a condition of living out the living God. This is because the house of God is the living God becoming flesh and being manifested in the flesh. In the four Gospels, God was manifested in the flesh in Jesus as a single individual. But in

1 Timothy 3, God's manifestation in the flesh is in the entire church corporately. Every local church should be a manifestation of God in the flesh. Hence, it is not enough just to have zeal and service. Our zeal and service must originate from spirit and life.

How do we know that our service is of spirit and life? This requires us to live the crucified life to be conformed to Christ's death and thereby manifest the power of Christ's resurrection from us. Furthermore, we need to let others see that we are those who live by the bountiful supply of the Spirit of Jesus Christ. Therefore, our living shows whether our service is of spirit and life. We must live in the shadow of the cross daily. I am not, but the Lord is—not I, but Christ. He is everything, and everything is of Him. Both in our daily living and in our activities in the meetings we need to be living and full of the Spirit. I feel that up to this day we still have not fully lived out the vision which we have seen of the Lord. All of us should be so living that before we come to any meeting, we begin to meet from our home by getting our spirit ready and by releasing our spirit. Once we get to the door of the meeting hall, we are singing; we sing while climbing up the stairs, we sing while going to our seat, and we sing even after sitting down.

In the meetings there is the need for the elders to take the lead, but all they need to say is that today we want to first read Ephesians 4. This is good enough; there is no need to say more. You do not need to tell the saints how to read the Scriptures, how one section should read one verse and another section read the next verse. After the brothers and sisters hear that the reading is in Ephesians 4, a young sister may pray before the reading begins, saying, "Lord, we really thank You for another wonderful meeting. We are here to read Your holy Word; in Your holy Word there is life and light. We pray that You would release Your life and light again." A young brother may add something, saying, "O Lord, Your word is Yourself. Therefore, when we read Your Word today, we are reading You." Then someone may stand up to read Ephesians 4:1, and after he finishes the reading, others may begin to pray-read. Our meetings should be living to such an extent. All that is required is for the elders to make a simple announcement, and the rest should come out in a living way.

However, most of our meetings in the churches have not been freed from the dead and depressed condition of Christianity. It is not easy to overthrow such a condition. This has to start with us. First we need to be living, and then we need to stir up others and make them living. We need to do this until all the churches are so living. We need to take the cross and live by the power of the resurrection of Christ through the bountiful supply of the Spirit of Jesus Christ.

THE NEED FOR BLENDING

Lastly, the churches also need the blending. Today due to the progress in telecommunications and means of transportation, the geographic distances have been greatly reduced. Prior to World War II, it was not easy for people to travel from the United States to Hong Kong. Because of the different modes of transportation and difficulties of travel, people could not arrive and be gathered together at the same time. If so, how could there be the blending? However, there are so many airplanes flying throughout the whole world; they are speedy and punctual. Today all kinds of inventions and instruments have caused the people in the entire world to be blended. The blending of the Body of Christ is possible through all the modern means of transportation. Hence, all the churches should live in life and in the spirit and be blended with one another for the manifestation of the reality of the Body of Christ.

How marvelous that the Lord raised up His recovery in China and then brought His recovery to the different places of the world through the changes in the world situation and the various scientific inventions! What the Lord has done is truly wonderful. We all need to catch up with the Lord's move and cooperate with Him for the fulfillment of His heart's desire in eternity.